Contents

Listen!

Meow!

A cat rubs your leg.

It wants to be petted.

Little Pebble™

Our Pets

Cats

by Lisa J. Amstutz

raintree

a Capstone company — publishers for children

Raintree is an imprint of Capstone Global Library Limited, a company incorporated in England and Wales having its registered office at 264 Banbury Road, Oxford, OX2 7DY – Registered company number: 6695582

www.raintree.co.uk
myorders@raintree.co.uk

Edited by Marissa Kirkman
Designed by Juliette Peters (cover) and Charmaine Whitman (interior)
Picture research by Morgan Walters
Production by Laura Manthe
Originated by Capstone Global Library Limited
Printed and bound in India

ISBN 978 1 4747 5714 0 (hardback)
22 21 20 19 18
10 9 8 7 6 5 4 3 2 1

ISBN 978 1 4747 5427 9 (paperback)
23 22 21 20 19 18
10 9 8 7 6 5 4 3 2 1

British Library Cataloguing in Publication Data
A full catalogue record for this book is available from the British Library.

Acknowledgements
We would like to thank the following for permission to reproduce photographs: Getty Images: KidStock, 5; Shutterstock: 5 second Studio, top 7, Africa Studio, bottom 21, ANURAK PONGPATIMET, top 21, Bogdan Sonjachnyj, left 9, Borja Laria, right 9, fantom_rd, 15, Grey Carnation, 17, ILonika, bottom 7, ka pong26, 11, Kalmatsuy, back cover, MaraZe, 19, MNStudio, Cover, Mr Aesthetics, (wood) design element throughout, Okssi, left 13, Seika Chujo, 1, Yimmyphotography, top 13

Every effort has been made to contact copyright holders of material reproduced in this book. Any omissions will be rectified in subsequent printings if notice is given to the publisher.

All the Internet addresses (URLs) given in this book were valid at the time of going to press. However, due to the dynamic nature of the Internet, some addresses may have changed, or sites may have changed or ceased to exist since publication. While the author and publisher regret any inconvenience this may cause readers, no responsibility for any such changes can be accepted by either the author or the publisher.

Cats make other sounds too.

Happy cats purr.

Angry cats hiss.

All about cats

Some cats have long hair.

Other cats have short hair.

Cats lick their hair

to keep it clean.

Some cats are one colour.

Calico cats have patches.

Their hair is orange,
white and black.

Tabby cats have stripes.

calico

tabby

Cats have claws on their toes.

They scratch often.

This keeps their claws sharp.

claws

13

Cats have some very good senses.

They see well in the dark.

Cats can hear well too.

They feel with their whiskers.

Growing up

Look!

It is a litter of kittens.

They drink milk

from their mother.

After four weeks,

kittens eat cat food.

Yum!

Playful pets

Cats like to play with you.

They chase toys.

This cat hides in a box.

Peek!

Glossary

angry feeling of being upset and unhappy

claw hard curved nail on an animal's paw

hiss to make a "sss" sound like a snake

kitten young cat

litter group of animals born at the same time to one mother

meow noise a cat makes

purr to make a low, soft sound

sense way of knowing about your surroundings; hearing, smelling, touching, tasting and sight are senses

whisker long stiff hair growing on the face and bodies of some animals

Read more

Cats: Questions and Answers (Pet Questions and Answers), Christina Mia Gardeski (Capstone Press, 2017)

First Book of Cats (Bloomsbury Animals Collection), Isabel Thomas (A&C Black, 2014)

Kitty's Guide to Caring for Your Cat (Pets' Guides), Anita Ganeri (Raintree, 2014)

Websites

www.bbc.co.uk/cbeebies/topics/pets
Discover a variety of pets, play pet games and watch pet videos on this fun BBC website.

www.bluecross.org.uk
Find out more about how to choose a pet and care for your pet on the Blue Cross website.

Comprehension questions

1. Would you like to own a cat? Why or why not?

2. Why is it important for cats to scratch?

3. What does a calico cat look like?

Index